TORCH
RIVER

TORCH
RIVER

ELIZABETH
PHILIPS

Brick Books

Library and Archives Canada Cataloguing in Publication

Philips, Elizabeth
    Torch River / Elizabeth Philips.

Poems.
ISBN-13: 978-1-894078-57-3
ISBN-10: 1-894078-57-8

I. Title.

PS8581.H545T67 2007   C811'.54   C2006-906535-7

We acknowledge the Canada Council for the Arts, the Government of
Canada through the Book Publishing Industry Development Program
(BPIDP), the Saskatchewan Arts Board, and the Ontario Arts Council
for their support of our publishing program.

Cover photograph by Elizabeth Philips.
Author photograph by Doris Wall Larson.

The book is set in Sabon and Stone Sans.

Design and layout by Alan Siu.

Brick Books
431 Boler Road, Box 20081
London, Ontario N6K 4G6

www.brickbooks.ca

for D. and J.

It isn't such a bad thing,
to live in one world forever.
—James Galvin

Contents

PART FOUR

Breath

Who's to say this life isn't the eternal life?
The no-time, the hover between in-
and exhale—both wellspring
and spur—is the source of the extra strength
you use to loosen the screw that holds down
everything,
                    or this morning, the heft I need
to shuttle from boulder to boulder
over the slump of rock meant to keep the riverbank
from moving.
                    Each day, small increments,
ratchetings of the essential force
are summoned up
from nowhere:
                    that pause, before the expulsion
of breath, is the pivot you turn on
when you turn and walk away, saying
nothing, not giving them
the satisfaction.
                    It's that little catch, of pleasure
or release, when I first glimpse the river
each morning, the river that never pauses, not
in its meander or undertow, the light
breaking apart the sky and reassembling it
                    beyond
the wide, flat rock we call
Pelican Rock.
                    As you can see
one sits there now, absurdly large,
unimaginable. Her lower jawbone, wire
thin, lifts the vast skin of her pouch, gullet

cum fishnet, at this moment empty.

What was I saying?

Something about the caesura, the stillness that isn't
the gathering in

or the letting go.

A thought
so slippery it flits away, following my glance
into the water, where I imagine it

taking shape,

fish-like, exploring the grooved and rolling
river bottom, becoming more
detailed, clearer

as the bird looks—

or so it seems—my way.

And now I wait on shore: whatever I was thinking
is out there and will be recaptured, returned, or
vanish,

diluted by the massive flow, the irresistible
on-goingness,

in this instance what we call
the South Saskatchewan.

What's everlasting must be—

do you think?—that instant that is neither
in nor out, when you do not breathe
but rest, at the point of turnaround, full
stop,

infinitesimal yet loaded, densely

particulate, containing every thought
you've ever had—

            had and lost
—until now.

         Until the bird slowly opens
her great wings and strokes the air, three
long beats, and she is airborne, rowing
with ponderous grace
downstream.

               Who's to say
this life is not the eternal life.
Breath in,

breath out—

PART ONE

Before

In the woods an hour ago,
I found bearberry—
do you remember what they call
kinnickinnick? Of course
you remember. The small
sticky leaves clinging to my face,
that summer, years ago, when I came up
from beneath you.
                    This was before
any of the catastrophes.
We were far from innocent,
but we were, yes,
                    unknowing.
Your body shines, glistens, in memory,
as you lie back on the bed of moss
and I approach, bare feet wet from the lake,
and kneel. I look up once
at the backdrop of white spruce
and resinous wind, and look down,
and cover you.

A line returns now, a fragment
from what I tried to write
afterwards: *you
can only get there by water.*
I still hope to use it, to play
with how it breaks:
                    *you can only
get there by water.* I'll punctuate this
with the real and the imagined.
I can clearly see how the leaves

on my cheeks became green-flecked
motes in your eyes
                    and then in mine.
And you alone know the texture and shade
of moss beneath my hips, the foliage
over my shoulder, and how
the wind insinuates between us
when we draw apart, as we wade
into the shallows, warm and cool
and warm.
                    We pull on our clothes
while we're still wet, stepping into the boat
and pushing off. How buoyant we were
for days after.
                    I'm going to say it now,
are you listening? You can only get there
by water.

Lake Aubade

I back-paddle, reversing, glissando, out
into the bay, expansive mantle of sky
in my wake. Morning still folded
inside its smoky envelope, the lake-face
opening with each stroke, showing
its ribs of sand, stone throat, clotted
palate.
      The boat is aligned
with my line of sight, the wind leans
on the offside and the pattern
is set:
      j-stroke, power stroke,
glide—

ↀ

Farther out, the depths
are deceptive, the lake could be
an abyss, or
      all surface,
thin as the lens of meniscus
on a glass of water.

I stare down into that green
galaxy, thinking with each torque
of the blade:
      I don't know, I don't know,
I don't know.

ↀ

The lake gives way, the flutter of its oh-so-pliable
skin a thoughtful fingering of notes up and down
the metal hull.

              I want to consider the formal
elements of morning, the sky implied
by a faint spiral of cloud, but otherwise
                            blank, an unmarked
folio, and the conifers hemming
the shore, their better selves
growing down, crowning softly
underwater, dream-like, the lake showing us how
            to loosen, how to forgo
definition,
       the storyline
                   forever breaking up, dissolving
into questions. Where are we
now? What comes next?

                 ❧

Black ducks bead the horizon, lifting the line
as they rise, scarcely leaving the water then
resettling, silver links of nubile light
undulant between them, impossible
to count or quantify...

I trail after them, slow arc
of the paddle underwater as I practice
stealth, *diminishment*,
hoping to vanish like the scar
where the diving gull's beak entered,
wresting a fish up and away, metallic

tail flapping like a third and broken
                         wing. The cut water,
after a few breaths, reconciled,
                             quiet
as before.

             ॐ

A loon appears to the leeside, her ululating
call, half laughter, half
despair, as she signals with
wing-beat and water walk, a sashaying
liquid poise, spelling,
                    intruder, intruder.
I reach out to sweep
myself out of her way and the boat spins
like a compass: north, northwest, south,
southeast,
          north: an infinity
of directions. *Choose, choose
now*, the loon low in the water, the night
           an ashy sheen
on the undersides of the waves.

             ॐ

A flock of geese engines over
in a syncopation of wings,
jazzy,
       dactylic, almost
danceable,
          the sky in their wake

chalky, smooth, the waves talking
of nothing but going on, *lip-lip,*
lip-lip,
   and then the anticipated
change-up as the boat rounds the island, the wind
easing, the sun, a flickering
       corona, implicit,
on the verge of rising.

    ∾

Where the heron flies, high overhead, the sun
is in the clear, the parabolic
body of the bird catches it, an intimation of blue
in a controlled glide southwest.
        From horizon to horizon
its wings move, slowly, once,
      twice,
as if
  hurry, urgency, need,
were antithetical to the morning
air,
       to flight.

    ∾

To the north, terns fly in cross patterns,
back and forth over the water,
     a sinuous,
energetic
   flux, restless as
free electrons,

                    and for an instant as I slide
beneath them, I'm the nucleus,
                              encircled
in a sketchy chaos,
                        intricate, impromptu,
their paths
            unmappable.

                    ❧

As the sun crests, I paddle farther
east, chasing it back behind the pines
and tamarack,
                    and coast there, on the spine
of the almost present
day, the snaking
                    diamondback,
until the light overtakes and claims me, claims my
                    shadow, a sudden
steely cast
            on the water.

                    ❧

The earth takes me back,
restoring the awkwardness of first
steps—a displaced
buoyancy in my hips as I haul the boat,
braced on thighbones, five feet up
the beach—
and I'm not quite
                    balanced, like some new

animal,
        a dissevered
water boatman—

Walking away from the grey hull
upturned on the grass,
                pitted keel
flecked with water and sand, the sun,
slipping free of the lake,
                is low-slung
but keen,
        a needling
breath on the back of my neck.

Jackknife/1

On the beach, I am who I imagine
I am, a boy
alone. I work

at skipping stones, Sunday
in early autumn, along the vacant
shoreline. Waves coil and uncoil,

frothing along the pebbled
strip of sand. Here, I have all I need—
glimmer of the other

shore, suspended slash of blue,
eighteen miles across—
and all I want

is within reach,
a good throwing arm, and no one to watch
as I practice, flick, flicking

my wrist, honing the degree of spin
and distance. Hours of twist
and pitch, twist and pitch,

and I believe I've perfected
the sidearm, and pleasure
is a wing of stone

and at least seven short flights, ricocheting
off the water, before it hits a wave
and sinks.

In every season, I unleash myself
here. In winter, tectonic plates of ice
lock the water in—layer on layer

of panes, four feet of ice,
too thick to see through
to the underworld

of perch and goldeye, catfish
and sunfish, drowsing
blades of light.

And in spring, the frozen monolith
collapses into floes of broken teeth.
One day at the edge of this decaying

surf, I find a dead frog, swollen
three times its natural size, nothing like
the frog I caught where the creek

empties into the lake, and dissected
on the kitchen table one summer afternoon
when no one was home.

The ice-frog is a balloon of khaki
skin, inflated by some inner
explosion, poisonous

and slow. But the frog on the table,
sacrifice to wonder, revealed
inside its belly

a nest of jewelled
organs, like the innards of a living
watch. I buried it

at the end of the yard,
shaken by my grief at its unwinding,
at how the scalpel had taken

a world of pearled cogs and slick
synapses, the jumping
heart,

and transformed it
into a slack green glove.

Harbour

The dock that smells of fish scales and creosote
is awash in four-foot waves, silty

slopes of water sweeping up
and over, sawing at my bare legs

beside the rocking fishermen's skiffs, cradled
in their creaking ropes, the wind

in freefall. I wade half the length of the pier
before the iron railings disappear, nothing ahead

but open water, an undertow of fear
reeling me to shore, as I tell myself the story

of the boy who didn't turn back,
who fell in and was lost

and the whole town mourned him.
I race away from the harbour

along the beach, the retreating waves stinging
my feet as I run, thrilling to the current

of wilderness in the blowing sand
and lashing water:

to fight to the last
and then surrender and drown, and be home

by five. Head bowed for grace,
I am the shy daughter

and the son, wind-burnt and radiant
in disguise.

Jackknife/2

Each day, I am apprenticed to the boy
I want to be.

He rifles the ball
and I catch it

or I fumble.
His red head ducks and weaves,

thinking, *end zone.*
I tag him

or I don't.
He swaggers

no matter what.
With the deftness

of a novice
I've learned the language

that drives us
toward that hallowed

and to no mind
imaginary

goal line.
Fuck! is the sound of

the ball,
well-kicked, or a pass,

snagged
out of the achingly fresh

October air.
The boy I want to be

is the one who slams me
into the chain-link fence

(nascent breasts
like crushed buds)

because I won't
stay on the sidelines,

cheering,
or skip rope and sing

with the other girls
in the lee of the school.

~

One day I make
a lot of *great saves*,

the next, I'm a *sieve*,
always on

defence, I risk a swing
at the schoolyard bully,

we wrestle in the snow
till the bell rings,

and I don't *cave*,
and for the next week

I'm a hero.
She can take that guy,

the refrain goes
from mouth to mouth.

I learn to scowl
even in the class photo,

I'm thinking
act natural,

as in a novel
by Zane Gray.

My horse is black,
my Stetson white,

come sunset, I'll be riding
into it.

Stormy Weather

The book has been bent
out of shape by the rain.

I'll never be the same
again. On the lake

the rain seems to be rising
into cloud. Inside the book

the words won't run
if I hold them under my wing.

If I hesitate long enough, just
looking around,

the boat may fill
with water, the rain

coming down so fast
I'll sink without knowing it.

Blue water, grey water,
tempest, palimpsest,

a hissing infinity of
kisses. So many

ways, so many waves
goodbye and hello.

The waters converge
and the book falls apart.

This lake's the farthest thing
from an idyll.

Meanwhile,
the shore approaches

a few boat lengths
and I'll be born

again. I'll pass over,
from the world of blur and swoon

and into the world where standing
is still, at least

until the wind becomes
a wilderness

and asks for my clothes.
If I understood the wind

everything
would be revealed.

For now, I'm paddling hard,
I am the rain's instrument,

and it's driving me
home, which is, I believe,

neither there
nor here.

Reprise

My feet force the earth to move,
propelling the slope east as I plumb, step by step,
the slithering lip of ravine, searching out
the river trail.
                        Is this the right direction?
After three days of rain, housebound,
I'm disposed to qualms, shaking off the sleep
of not thinking, of being
bound,
            skin by skin
by skin,
                to you, our mouths
searching, mine on yours, and yours
on mine. When the sky opens,
I'm blind, stumbling
along a chasm of light, the sun
                                    all green
sizzle
        in the many-mirrored fronds,
the shag of horsetail and dripping
ferns.
            Is this the right direction? away from
the path we followed last night, through the smooth
sheets and onto the floor?
                            I stagger, doubtful, down
the bank, careening sideways for traction
on the sodden grass, one hand on the cut and torrent-
torn shoulder—this carrying and being carried
away by water, such heavy
work. What else

can I bring home to you? This brief
shattering sun, and columbine
about to bloom, to name itself by opening
its five rosy doves

                          above the savage, rain-fed
current, spooling north
                                into the next meander.
I turn back as the clouds draw in, shading
my tracks. And I can see
                          this is the way
back.
        Rain on the roof, wind
making the house rise: stormy weather,
we'll embrace it from the inside, rolling
together, under and over and
under,
        in the wet seam.

PART TWO

The Hanging Tree

Yesterday, your hair smelled of green tea, and so like smoke
I followed you from the living room
to the bedroom, and would have stayed
but my mother called
about the horse,
                        she said she was okay until Dad led him
from the barn and across the pasture, and past
the hanging tree.
                        That's when she turned away
from the window.
The neighbour was there with his backhoe, she could hear
the machine still running.
                        But for some things
you can't prepare.

Afterwards, I carried
a few books upstairs, whatever I wanted
nearer to hand—John Donne, the field guide
to Prairie grasses, and several
unread novels.
                        Oh well, it doesn't get any easier,
my mother's voice
came with me, back to where you lay,
undressed now, and
waiting.
                        In the time intervening, I'd almost
forgotten you.
                        The horse
had an abscessed tooth and his ribs were staves.
                        I reached across

and touched your hair, nothing like the grass
that fuelled his life. The pit was wide
and deep
        to keep the coyotes out.

Later, you drifted off, your breath
furrowing down
        and into
the afterlife of pleasure,
            while I hung on a little longer
to the scented sheets, thinking sleep
insufficient, a poor metaphor for what used to be called
eternal rest. That I'd get up in the morning,
and go to my desk, and try again to earn
my passage, to see all things
            equally: the fallen
horse (his head so much heavier now), my father's
grimace as he shakes the neighbour's hand,
as he walks around, not over, the square of newly broken
earth,
    and the wind, as it always is
just there, gentled
by the big spruce, and sweet, redolent with twenty years
of spilled grain and dung and dust.

Nocturne

When I was small, it was always night
when I frightened my mother with a sound
I made, a harshness of breath
that wasn't a cough, more like a straining
of water through stones,

                    or a lungful
of bees.

          For years I believed
that lost breath—my closing,
ossified throat—

               hadn't frightened me.
Until this morning, when I heard that same
frictive throttle in another's chest,
as my lover's father lay dying,

                   old heart
heaving, all the water left in his body
a sponge he must draw

                each breath through.
And this morning, it slipped
past me, the moment the moving ribs
fell still, the line between then
and now

        so nearly nothing, a low mist
subsiding, shadow
of a shadow.

              And on the evening of the day
of his death, I bow towards
that child in her bed, caught in the furious
work of inspiration, her rasping
like the thrashing inside
a chrysalis,

and I am my own
mother, risen to tend her daughter
in the night.

Child, I say, bending over her
in the haze of steam from the kettle,
in the lamplight,
            little moth of smoke,
open your eyes
and tell me what you know.

Drift

I walk through the house. I stand before doors
never seen before.
                        I'd remember, don't you think?
this one, deep yellow, or that, with its knotted
black panelling. In the mirror at the end
of the hall, a face swims, pierced
by its outward gaze,
                        and the light
filtering in, in its borrowed
robes.

I drift toward the window, so far away
down the corridor, the window I stood at
hours ago, overlooking the garden and its forest
of lilies. I hang back, wary of this
threshold, its deceptive
                        transparency.
And as I approach I'm stricken
by the day, by how much the season
has altered,
                        the snow between the fences
piled higher than the famous snows
of childhood. I glide closer, and my breath
scalds the pane, silver
emissary:
                        the inside
seen from the inside. And my other form,
the one sewn out of fog, escapes
into the thorny arms of the Russian Olive,
into the wings of a small bird, fluttering there

like a stitch out of time. Its call
is a papery sound, not entirely
confident, the bird
in its blue hood, in its body
of grey threads.
                    Another breath
and it's away, flickering
out of sight. How the streets it passes over
will appear, I can't begin
to guess. Last night, they were as bare
as old bones, and annealed
with ice.

I have to ask, which door
is my door?
                    No matter, I trust
it won't open with a simple twist.
I'll have to use both hands.
                    Sinister, dextrous—
between the two I might fiddle
the lock and ease my way
from this house

to this house.

The Hall Closet

She pushes the doors apart and they disappear
into the walls, and on the upper shelves
at the back, a row of grey boxes, and inside
old letters, bills, official-looking
documents.
                    She's inhaled their fragrance
of abandonment, fingered their compressed
folds. She's read them haphazardly, reaching
blindly in and lifting out a letter on frail blue
paper or a bill from the doctor for a late night
call.
            She knows she shouldn't delve
so freely—the boxes are closed, hidden
almost. On the lower shelves, in plain
view, the games are stacked,
                                        dominoes,
rummoli, chess, decks of cards—everything
a child needs to learn the knack of winning
and losing, to practice
deception.
                    She stands, undecided, peering in—

the letters sleep in their boxes, endlessly repeating,
Dear Jane, My Dear Jane, My dear...
The garden needs hoeing. How are the children?
How is your garden? William is working
too hard. The news, today, terrible. The long
winter and more snow again last night.
Spring is upon us now, a flood
of slush and water.

                    Standing below
and looking up, she can hear them, the echoing
phrases, and she tries again to guess the meaning
behind the script.
                    What news? How late
did he return each night, eyes haggard,
mouth down-turned? What did he do, afterward,
in his small attic room, with its many clocks
and bare, pocked walls?
                         She's weary of inventing
gestures—the face of disdain or envy, the sharp
words of disaffection—

                         weary of the pictures
she cannot complete, the missing pieces
that may explain why this man never had
a lover, why that woman chose, with iron
conviction, her singular ways.

She's had it with games, each round the same
obstacles and openings, the same blue
and red board and clattering dice, plastic
figures marching in a circle.
                         Each hand is lucky
or it isn't. The cards refuse to add up
until a sudden flush, a rich configuration
of faces and the short-lived
                         rush, the sweetness
of besting others. Aggravation,
war, crazy eights, concentration,
trouble, sorry. Words
                    that no longer tempt her,

even when they arise in the letters, signalling
the shift from the good news to the bad,
the confident hand flowing toward
but never arriving at
                        this day, this hour.

And there's no end to the possible
variations. Whether she cuts and deals
or discovers a missing page, an outright
declaration of love or remorse,
                                questions hover
after the boxes are shoved back
out of sight. No matter which way
she turns, no future is certain, no outcome
foretold.
            Not wanting to play
and not wanting to pry, she draws the doors
in, they sigh as they connect, the mild
wood fair as skin
                    and blank. What she wants
is a passageway to a new country,
where she can walk farther and farther
inland, seeking food, seeking water,
and finding
                first a stream, and days and days
later, a river.

Jackknife/3

The night we go swimming in the harbour,
in the dusk of a retreating
storm, he and I,

and three others take turns
diving from the pier
in the still simmering

convected air. Over the lake
spent clouds, to the west, terns
crying above the white-washed

warehouse walls.
We line up again and again
in our dripping suits, water

ticking down our legs as we praise
and mock each dive. Until he, grinning,
climbs onto the roof

of a fisherman's boat,
and I follow. On the slippery wood,
shoulder to shoulder, one deep

breath, and we jackknife,
the twin blades of our shadows
falling together

into the water. He comes up first
and lunges, fighting
to hold me,

muscle to muscle,
under, and we're dropping into
who knows what

on the lake bottom, decades of lost
nets and fishing line, the spectre
of the diver hooked years ago

on a loop of rusted wire.
I kick back and away from him,
scissoring up into the adrenalin-

blue sky. And I'm out
and on the pier and pelting him
with stones as he swims hard

for the main dock, a hundred strokes,
the others' laughter echoing
across the oily mouth of the harbour.

And since that evening of flight, of darkness
and ascent, I am always on his side
in the game.

And the lake was blood-warm,
as it often is
after rain.

Double Dare

You still have the knife
so it must have happened.

But you didn't find it, half-buried
on the beach, that was just a story

for the adults.
You and your friends, all boys,

playing at some version of tag
among the dry-docked

whitefish boats. Clambering aboard
The Bluebell, you jump

from stern to stern. A sharp wind
off the ice

tailing you. Break-up
soon, but today is white

to the horizon.
You can see clearly

through the small cabin window
to where the knife

hangs on a nail.
The door opens

for your shoulder and the scraped
knuckles of your hand

reach for it.
On the deck, you stand, legs braced

as if against the buck and wallow of
the chop. You're caught,

entranced by the wheel you've made
from air. Flipping the knife

end over end in the glaring
light, the honed edge blurring as your fingers

reach into the spinning spokes of handle-
-and-blade,

and pull the knife out,
safely, each time.

Until the smallest boy
taps your shoulder, and you catch

cold metal. After you've sheathed
the knife, you pivot and dive,

tagging him, red thumbprint
on the back of his jacket

and he's it
for the rest of the day.

To Keats

I lie in bed reading *The Pocket Book of Verse*,
      discovered between Dickens and Jack London
on a basement shelf, its stained, 1940 flyleaf
      signed by my mother in watery
schoolgirl script. The book opens with excerpts
      from the Bible. I leaf ahead to Tennyson,
to the anguished garden of Amy Lowell.
      Fourteen and restless, I'm trying not to
dwell on the scornful look of a girl who doesn't know
      how much or how often I parse her every
phrase. She loves me not, I think, flipping past
      Wordsworth's daffodils.

In a well of lamplight I fall into Keats
      for the first time—*how to load and bless*
with fruit—the lines ripening, my hands beneath
      the sheets, moist bud
engorging as I try not to see her with
      her boyfriend, his farm-boy fists
on the wheel, his eyes grazing
      her hemline as he fishtails down rutted
winter streets. I glance up as wind
      shakes panes coated with frost,
making the moonlight more silver, and less
      like a gleaner thou dost keep.
But what I sink into is the sorrow of *the soft-dying*

day, its footing in the raw grief, the yellow
      clay. I read the poem again and again,
inflamed, always on the brink, then slipping back

into the book, Keats's slinky brocade
all over me like a net of raw silk, *as the light wind
lives or dies*, while an implacable
prairie winter cracks the floor joists, the killing cold
never heavier. Until I'm released
into the mystery of the ending, when a squall
of swallows infests the sky
above the river shallows.

Waking next morning, I'm heavy-headed, drugged
by dreams of summer, and turning over
my mother's book I vow to learn each flourish,
as if by a feat of memory, I might shame
my longing into defeat and lock in the essence
of that first reading, that innocent
passage from line to line. Each night I am at work,
my tongue a nib, a feather
in my throat as I whisper, recomposing,
until by spring I own *The Pocket Book of Verse*
and I'm hoarse with almost knowing, almost
breaking through.

PART THREE

Lullaby

Here you lie, never more
mortal, never more lithe
than after love,
                    sleep
condensing, sweet
in your mouth, wrists
and ankles cooling,
the arches of your feet
released as light bends
in the clefts at elbow
and knee, and in the slip
where I have
                    and have
and have been.
Your hand, now,
on my thigh, palm open:
                    my beloved,
adrift, and almost gone.
If this is a glimpse
of the afterlife, then I'm
with you,
                    I surrender
as we float, a living
raft, pulse tied
to pulse,
both of us near
and both of us far.
                    Here,
on the cusp
of dreaming, the wind

lisps across the sill
and the longed-for rain
comes down
                    and down,
scattering the dust
from the dreamt and the un-
dreamt leaves.

Belief

If I can give you the morning, grey, early
spring, the morning of the day the woman rises
out of the very bed where he last
breathed,
        rises after a sleep of two
deaths, in a thin yellow nightdress,
the heat turned down, the furnace
cold.
    If I can deliver you
into her gesture, the right hand hanging
and the left tucked
          into her neckline, nesting
there, as she stands between the stove
and the table.
        And here are the floorboards
beneath her feet, and the smell in the house,
which is the scent of less, of almost nothing.
           Can you hear
what she's thinking?
She's about to look for the loaf of bread
she believes is in one of the cupboards
or behind the dishes stacked on the counter.
If I can find you in her,
         in the faint
that strikes her, a weakness that is hunger
and more than hunger,
         as her weight drops
into her hands on the dark wood of the table,
palms down to catch herself
        as she falls

with the blood in her arms
into her hands and through them and into
the grain, where it is not spring, or morning,
but late, and no buds
                              awaken, no green stirs
and swells.
              If I can find a way,
if I can winnow out a word
that will let you in,
                      it may be *green* or *palms*
or *nightdress*.
              I can wait.
                              I have some time,
I can't say how much—
                      but I have her
in mind, and I'm hoping
that will be enough.

The Promise

Everyone coming into her room can see it.
      Against the north fence, beneath
           the cottonwood, catching the sun—

a new garden seat, wrought iron, pristine,
      filling up, this morning, with snow.
           Spring, an indefinite

length of time away. And this room, like each
      in the house, a sick room, pill bottles
           on the nightstand, vials

on the mantel. And that hush, as her family
      gathers in the hallway, tendering
           into the forced calm

their questions, their wavering answers. Her flesh
      thin and thinning, counted against
           their hopes.

In her room, she stares out at the white day,
      seeing herself on the sun-warmed
           bench, red lilies behind her.

What she can no longer imagine is walking in easy
      strides across the grass, that green
           infinity. Can she endure

the coming changes? Snow turning to rain, rain
      sparking leaves, those lime-coloured
           lashes of new life.

She watches the clouds, a flourishing of pure cold
    rushing east to west as the snow
        falls faster, blurring

fence boards and gnashing boughs, as the wind
    flies through the iron leaves
        that face her window.

The Widow

She looks in the mirror and doesn't know herself.
           She's lost so many pounds, someone
the size of a small child is gone, and she misses
           the weight. She fills her bath
with a froth of white foam to cover
           the sallow wishbone of her pelvis.
She closes her eyes when she washes
           her breast, the soap slick and cool,
and sister to it, the scar that runs, unnerved,
           across her chest, a hollow
where he used to rest his head. And she pauses
           there, her heart on the other side
of that line, and she doesn't know how to hold
           in that splice the hum
of his absence. And yet she does.
           As she breathes, she remembers him.

Fatherhood

The First Hours

They walk through the streets into cave
after cave of blossoms, cherry and plum
and the ivory magnolias.

Whenever the pains come, he and she
embrace, marrying again
under such chapels. She leans

the spasming of her great belly
into the hollow beneath
his breastbone.

And afterwards, hooks his gaze
into hers, and her irises are water,
a blue he falls into like thirst, helpless

to draw back or look away, a drink
he has to take, swallowing
her murmured words and small

laughter, fear
arching in his side like a new rib.
As the rhythm of the pains

increases, they arrive back
at their door. He twists
the handle. Over his left shoulder

the sun, simmering in the west, is glazed,
red-rimmed,
and the sky is milk.

Night

And now it's midnight, or later,
their small house grown
smaller, the corners effaced

by darkness. One lamp
lights the room where she lies,
now on her side, now half-sitting

against high pillows, now
kneeling on all fours. Each contraction
longer than any moment

he's known, longer than days
and days of work, his fingers dull
on sheaves of papers, longer

than the weeks of laughter
with his friends that final summer,
or the deep trough of

pleasure, longer than his hunger
for her longing. And all through it
the bass note of her moan, its ripening

tremolo as the pain
rises, then ebbs away, undertow of
gravitas, swelling

turbulence she climbs,
her low wail a chain
dragging in the wake of a boat.

He lies behind
and against her, holding ice
to cool the cramping

back labour. Hour
circles hour, the room hushed,
breathless, then

a brightening, a film of white
at the window, the city
he's forgotten, the street,

the flowering fruit trees, the colours
of the other rooms,
tremor on the line, his mother's

questions late last night.
He's almost forgotten his child, its urgent
descent, has lost the picture

on the screen
in the doctor's office, waving
coral of its fingers.

Sighing, she struggles up to sip
water through a straw.
He nuzzles her bare shoulder, tastes

the sheen of salt
on salt, smells her hair, its spicy
oil. She speaks so

precisely now. *Water*,
she says, or *heat*, or *lower*.
Her eyelids flicker but do not open.

It's morning. He hears
someone switch off the lamp.
Another day. He tries to calculate

the duration, which is more
like distance—twenty
hours, or twenty-five? The numbers

don't add up. The midwife taps
his shoulder, takes his place,
ordering him

into the kitchen for food.
Through the back door, the scent of white
lilacs, and he's spinning

in the perfumed and dazzling
early air.
The counter is stark

with sun. The butter
glows yellow in a blue dish.
He balances

a slice of bread on his palm,
the pattern, like pores
in skin, of its dense

grain. He folds it
into a fist
and eats.

Day

There's almost no break now, between waves, her muscles
rivering, concentric,
the midwives far away, between her knees
on the quilt. And he doesn't know
what their gestures mean, the calm
orchestration of hands as they counsel her
to breathe
and rest, breathe
and rest.

They listen, after each contraction, to the child's heart.
The instrument cupped like an ear against the wall of skin,
they hear the magnified beating, it floods
the room, and below his feet the floor boards
seem to be trembling.

He moves from her side
to the couch behind her, cushioning her
between his legs. She holds
in the crush of her grip the bones of his hands.
In the channel, the narrow shaft,
the head tunnels down
and down, until she cries
now, can I!?
and the midwife consoles, *no,
don't, not yet*, as the mouth that isn't wide,
that can't be, thins and thins, the younger
of the midwives massaging

the noose of flesh,
easing it more taut and yet more
open, until

yes, and *now,*
and she who has laboured for a day and
a night, and into the afternoon,
inhales,
three quavering breaths, cleaving
out of exhaustion and into the hidden
stores of fat and marrow,

and bears down,
the dark disc of scalp pulsing forward
and back, forward and back, with each impossibly drawn out
exhalation, and then
the crowning,

and there will never be any more pain

than this, her hands throttle his,
and leaning into the oars, she pushes and
pushes, drawing him with her into the water, it washes over them,
the head surging
through, someone saying, *through*
the cord, and he can't see or speak, but imagines
a wet, tangled rope around the small stem of neck
as she rows deeper, sinking
down, face flushed, blood of the withheld
breath gathering massive in shoulders

and breasts, back arched, the belly
empurpled, royal
with the strain of staying under. And finally
onto the quilt the entire length of head, shoulders, hands and feet
pours out in one sweep of water and blood
and the baby lies there, his daughter

blue and grey and asleep.

2:41 p.m.

and in that moment his voice
shatters into shards of
                              if
and *maybe*
                    and
                              maybe
not,
          while the others
kneel around the infant, calling,
fluting her name as if life may be
praised into being,
                         and he
the only one among them
stalled, mute, his belief
                              foundering,
the two midwives cajoling her
as they work, manipulating the small
pump like a hand-held
                              lung, inspiring her
with scant
                    teaspoons of air, his daughter's
mother calls and calls, and her mother
also and in the same voice
but darker,
and he,
          in this room of women
singing,
          as the tiny chest stutters

once, twice, he knows,
                             as the blue-grey skin
kindles
           to rose, he knows this—
as she wakens with a coughing
cry—
        that this
is what he has come for.

3:15 p.m.

The midwife hands to him
his child, her cheeks streaked with vernix
and blood, her small hands, creased
pink lilies.

He was so certain
she'd look like any other infant, red
sea-prune, the usual
newborn, but she's purely
herself, the skin on her temples
lucent, round skull
heavy, her eyes a tidal blue-
black.
        And she's looking
at him, as awake
as he is, and everything in the room around them
is new. Except

he believes he's seen her
somewhere before.

There you are, he says.
There you are.

Song to the Areola

hers is the sadness
of the twin who lived,
her pink more dun,
bloom under shadow

his kiss is light,
praising how she rose,
her flame to his
quick tongue,

but her grief tonight
is a form of sleep,
so he doesn't sing
but rests his cheek

along the scar
and lays his breath
along her breast, until,
island of dark

into dark, she fades,
and he shifts
to the pillow,
bending to fit

the shape he thinks
must be the sorrow
he fears to know
and longs to follow

Out

At home, and tired of the sweating
windows, all day long and no one calls,
and no one here now
                            to prevent her—
neither son nor daughter—
she opens the door and slips out.
Against the best advice,
out—

into the prevailing wind, the minus thirty
chill raking at her as she walks, her fever
a mask and a veil, down the hill
to the river in its skirt of ice, riveted
with ribbons of snow, and beneath,
what she wants, and listens for,
                            the concealed
northward flow.

Late light and low lying, and the snow
blowing aslant. From a distance, the trailhead
is a tear in the weave
of trees, which she can't quite believe in
until she's there, and the aspen part
and she's in,
            pale trunks barring
the city and the city's eyes.
                        The sun
lancing among the branches, its lace
stopped in the ribs of wolf
and true willow.

The cold
like an ether on the bones in her face.

Where the path careens down
to pace alongside the current, capped now
(though there must be open water,
she can hear its fitful
patter), and she walks on it, the ice
levered up onto the bank by the lethal
shrug of the current,
her boots a hollow sound on this beached
bridge:
      knock knock,
who's below?

Half a mile and she's breathless,
shoulder to shoulder with a lichenous
stump—
      winded
and of the wind—and easy
for the first time in days.
She looks to the far side:
               white fields,
white river, and sees, rising
from the floe, a shape, a large tail and sloping
gait, and she's sure:
      coyote—

he must have been lying on the ice
and now he's angling north, as she is,

breath slowed, the path narrowing
into brush so thick it belies these remnant
woods.
       And she's out again
into the open, and the coyote's there still,
ghosting her.

They continue, another quarter mile together
and apart, until the coyote veers inland,
into the vee of the creek bed, and is gone
into scrub.
       All the way, returning,
she weakens, her fever flaring
with the ache in her side, as dusk
sweeps into the valley, its smoke
hazing the trail, the sun abraded
to a wraith, a ring
           of frost, falling
behind her, and it will not
shadow her,
       will not give chase
or draw her in.

Below

The white-winged crossbills, in waves of frenzy
        and calm, come to feed on the tawny
               cones of the spruce. The snow

feeds on wind, the wind on the barely suspiring
        conifers. The storm makes the birds'
           red more vivid,

like a sudden visitation of sorrow
        or joy. Joy lies in the woman
            walking below, her listening

as the birds work the cones, tearing into
        summer's sweetness. She does not know
            if she has failed, but she has

mistaken the wild for another kind of hunger.
        In this first month of expanding light,
            she wants to eat, with such fierce

intent, the day's offering. To find the one source,
        and fall on it, nothing in mind
           but that. Satiation

as close to hand as the tree, the fruit, the low-
        flying sky. The few females, inconspicuous,
           an uncertain grey,

display on their crowns the imprint of sun.
        She does not know if it is a blessing
        or a stain.

Who walks below? Looked down upon from above,
        from the tree's peak, her human gaze
                shimmers, a pale

uplifted oval—of all the species, hers is the animal
        that bears through each hour
                such a tender face.

She yearns, even in winter, to touch with her palms
        the supple, overburdened branches,
                and to hear how clearly

birdsong moves inside silence, not breaking
        but parting it, as the wind does, harrowing
                the snow.

The Waiting Room

1/

the grey walls were once
another colour, she can't
tell what, sitting here
with the dream, turning
in her hands, her quilted
hat.
      the blue

ribbons, cut and scattered,
like a sign that she was meant
to follow. to unravel
the mysterious disappearance of ...
she forgets, except

for the sensation, sharp,
of their edges, their slippery
width.
        in her hands
the ribbons were supple, yet
nicked like blades her fingertips,
that this morning, on waking,
she found perfectly
healed.

in this room, waiting, she looks
into the pink of each of her nails
(hands kept
           strictly
in her lap), her fingers hooked,

some vestigial memory of an arduous
climb. she wants to
lift a hand, but refrains, she will not
cup, for warmth or relief,
her breast—no,
she'd rather sleep,
rather lie down among the ribbons,
hoping their slash of steeped blue
will gather, generous around her,
and deftly
          leap
back into her wrists.

2/

on the other side of the wall a tapping, then
a tap, the rush of water flowing
and stopping, followed by laughter, the doctor's,
the patient's, and a third voice, low, like a
fulcrum, balancing—
                    and she wants to open the door
to this room, and turn
                    and open the door
to that room,
          and be welcomed,
naturally, in.

3/

and who is her company in this

waiting? on the seventh floor,

unseen, unmet, in rooms that mirror

hers. between injections, visitors, calling

the nurse, sending away

trays of food, she drifts into these

other, parallel

privacies, these companion

deaths, unfolding within

hearing. she listens, and

doesn't. last

requests sigh through her.

nothing stays

but the colour of words,

the murmured questions

grey, the cough, a choking

sulphur yellow,

and eyes, closing,

closing,

white.

4/

ribcage,
slow boat

ribcage,
catheter

spine,
the painful

edges of the liver,
methadone

occipital bone,
neck,

icy wind
off the water

the light from the hallway,
the light from the window

ribcage, sternum
stone boat

how is that now?
a wet sponge,

swabbed
mouth, stubbed

tongue
slow, stone, slow,

how is that
now?

5/

the night is felted
with hands, his
                    leaf-like,
light on her wrist,
on her shoulder

and her own, restive,
always plucking at sheets,
blankets

and the nurses', brisk, firm,
straightening

the night leans on eyelids, temples
one breath,
                two breaths

big-jointed, the night
hums, thick with fever
and snow,
                sleep
an uprush, a clattering
of wings
                withdrawing to the horizon

palm on palm on palm
                        a laddering of, a
lowering of

night, giving way to
night, one

                breath

and the rest
giving way to,
                giving

the rest
to—

PART FOUR

Prelude

When she wakes in the night there are always
the two things: yesterday's path, its calculus
of miles to come and miles
gone. And the question
of the record—
                   will she outwalk
memory, and have to carry
in her mouth, under her tongue, an entire
geometry of signs: print and spore, elusive
traces along the calcareous slopes, growing sharper
and more readable as she descends
into wetland. The earth leavening

as it falls: peat and bog, the trail fat
with needles, the notes

she cannot write down.

~

She walks and walks and walks: she wants
to know, what is the third
thing?—walking
                  as divination, walking
as a way of conjuring the necessary
heat.
      Heat in the synovial
oil, in the solar plexus, heat

in the hinge   and lift,   hinge
and lift.

~

In truth, it is her blood
that walks, walks and
wakes her:

Black
       spruce, black
                 cottonwood,

night fever.

~

On the evening of the day of the great-horned
owl, its wings open in her shoulders, as breath
does. She lies down to sleep, and bars of light
and dark sail from green through shadow and into
                    green
at the back of her eyes.

~

Question: dressing in the morning, she watches
herself, considering,
                          where in her
                                          the knife, the ready
blade, the two quick
talons. She touches the calyx
of the areola, puckered clasp
holding fast the chilled fist
of nipple.

~

Question: where does tenderness
reside, in the big body

or the little body?

~

The little body is corpuscle, fascia, the interior shunts
and valves, a narrowing

at wrists, where the carpals
float, aligning and re-
aligning.

And deeper, the worker bees of the small
intestine:

        gratitude,

shame.

~

The big body: the long bones of the legs scissoring
forward, the largess of their gait
as she moves north then northwest, the forest
pacing the ridgeback, thinning along the perimeter of
swamp, and where the ground's been disturbed, saplings
muscling in on a meadow of ragwort
and slough grass.

Later, and lower, the path
flows down to willow, and willow
into water. The leaves, their frosted
undersides, are a fringe of thirst
drawn carefully across
                the multitude
of eyes.

~

The big body says: you
walk, you walk—*you*

walk.

~

The little body says:

[touch me].

~

all day the rhythmic subaqueous
roll, the hips, lubricious and
frictional   the falling and the
                              catching
faith and doubt, faith
and doubt: the heart
tempo—   and always the blue skein of sky
following   what the body calls
temple   a weaving of what is seen
with what is imagined.

~

What she sees: wolf scat matted with tufts of coarse
hair, twisted grass, bone chips. And what she
imagines: wolves, a heaviness of shoulder, a bulked-up
wariness loping in and out of balance
with hunger. And behind the alder
a bear in the huffing of wind, in the uprooted
duff.

What she sees: bear scat seeded with rosehips, blue-black
skins, chokecherry pits.

              And a single hind print
in the clay, as large as
her own.

~

The big body says: I am balsam spruce and balsam

poplar: I am the wayward boughs of the Jack

pine, I am the supple, the towering

Lodgepole.

~

The big body
is very often
mistaken.

~

Question: Is there a middle body, middle distance, meeting
of the parallax view? Is there any way to marry
the two, any way for them to stay
married?

~

The little body defers,
defers, dwelling in the quiver
between desire
and dailiness: the hands of caress
and arousal

are busy making soup, finding water,
ensuring that the fire

is out.
        Laying a palm
over the ashes.

~

In the night, the third thing
loosens, flies deeper

into the trees. She lies inside
the tent, inside

the windiness of
matter: sleeps in the slit

of stoma, under each
eyelid a leaf, moonlight,

aspen swaying
high up, tracking her, inhaling

the sheen of her sweat.
Falling back again, she dreams

she has at last been seen:
cougar eye, like a low-slung

window, or lucent
stone,

deer eye of river sand, dusk
as it closes over the metamorphic,

the uninscribed.

~

Each morning she swims out through the pelvic
gate: the farther the wider, the farther

the wilder. And by the seventh hour of the third day
she has become a staff of roses, each vertebra

unfolding, and
                     aloft.

~

She has left behind lover, sister, father,
mother, friend. She has flown from the city
of strangers, their tired, incidental
glances.

                And now, this
                              groundswell, the softening
waters of the perineum
                      and slubbed
thorn,
       the full and stinging tip,

unsheathed.

~

On the last page, she writes:

Found an abandoned ladder leaning against a tree.
Weathered rungs on bark, a step
no one still living
has climbed, old heartwood
inclining to new.

What she doesn't say: lamplight
laces her fingers like the watery gold of the owl's
night vision. Her hand crawling slowly
down the page. And after, a whiff
of oily smoke, the brief linger of extinguished
light, and then the stars

move closer. Staccato of branches
as she passes into
the fallow body, its hazy
drift:

and when the sparrows and thrushes
strike up just before dawn, she hears in the hollow
beneath her left ear, a sifting—of fallen
leaves or seeds
                    rustling
across a threshold.

                    And she finds that it is,
once again,
morning.

Passage

The body of the fallen tree is wholly
      clothed in green moss, the year-by-year
fire of its undoing. And this is what halts
      her, its pulsing phosphorous
glow. She lowers herself, her gaze level
      with the most delicate of seeds, fawn
-coloured eyes sprung from old bark.
      And stays there, coiled
in the forest's breath, humid with night
      rain: caught in the tangled understory
radiating from her wrists, its profuse
      invention: leaves like threads,
leaves like the tines of umbrellas, wetly
      amphibious. Her shadow
makes the green more green, deepens and
      sharpens it. She bends closer
to the velvet that eats in its gloved mouth
      the ten-years-dead
Jack pine. The tufts of moss sweep all
      one way, as if born into an unyielding
north wind. And behind the deadwood,
      and rooted in it, a robust
red and grey trunk, its grooved bark split
      by summer on summer of slow
elevation. She tips her head back, spine
      arching as she traces the skirl of branches
up to the sunlit crown. One palm across
      the hummock of moss, she braces against
the dizzying downdraft of sky, shoulder bones
      cradling head bone. She cannot imagine
beginning again, and yet she smells it, the birth-
      smell, vernix of decay, on which new growth

feeds. The mounded tree that was once this
　　　　tall, and lifted
its share of light, is now a tannic sponge, ripe
　　　　with rainwater and microbial
life. The wind rivers through the canopy
　　　　and the creaking, dead-and-dying trees
lean harder on the living. She sinks deeper
　　　　into her body, her weight
bearing down through the strength in her legs
　　　　into forest floor, while her skull
floats, a cloud, an occlusion between
　　　　the light above and the dark below.
Listening for footfalls, the stealth of approaching
　　　　bear or wildcat, she thinks: *This is where
the story begins*, but she can't imagine
　　　　how. Should she follow the path
east to the water, or the path west to the high
　　　　ridge? On the brink of opening,
or having opened, through the passage
　　　　of one breath and into
another, hands on the pelt
　　　　of moss, she is waiting to rise
and be taken.

Oxbow

This is the river that strayed, that slipped
aside, and, becalmed in its separate bed,
stayed,
        this is the river
that feeds the rushes, the slow reeds
and heron, the river that sleeps
in a circle, and clasps within it
an island of ten white spruce, a hundred
aspen,
        and a meadow
the span of an embrace
that we've claimed this afternoon
to lie in, face to face
on a weft of cast-off leaves,
                and above
your bare shoulders,
           the sky, acutely
blue, hooked
on the pale green fingers of stripped aspen—
where the river stands down,
you turn me like water
cleft from water,
          and I fall back
into my own body, as your body
                divides
and joins me,
        into the passing
and the held.

Sunday

She kneels over me (I watch),
she kneels over me (I watch)
the underside of tongue, the tipped
breast   creamy
blue-veined   and the unseen

(above us, on the night
screen, two women lying nipple to nipple)

I look up into
the darkening of the inner, the swell
and fill of the outer. The crease where

slicking up and down the length of
up and down
                    the length of
I slip over and around the sleek
knot   inside the influx of salt-

water (what is open   opens
all the wider   tensile   and
crimson)

Hand me,

hand
me. I don't speak but think it, and she
looks, I feel the heat of her looking, as more
and more closely, mouth

on mouth (the inside of
sea scent, oysters
kelp   lustrous
anemone)

I feel her breath and at last the first
taste
and the next and next   slick
flickering   and a sudden
roughening as she lowers
herself

and what is close
becomes closer.

I rise   she falls   I rise   she
falls   I rise   she—

hand in her   fingers on my
(a quickening of thickened, blurred
lips)

I slip inside   slip and
tuck, slip and
tuck, down and in and down and

eyes deep
into, my whole face deep
into   rising
in and down and

through   falling
through falling—the red and plum
and rose of the ripe and the over-
ripe, awash in

you, beside me, *you*.

Late Storm

This is a season of incongruities,
                    a shroud of snow and gulls
grieving overhead, the wind swelling
and falling,
                    from a distance, an elegant
abstraction:
                    white sky, black water, white
ground. But here, in the throes of it, the cold
is an existential problem, a too real
intensity.
                    The far riverbank rides in and out
of view, unharboured.
                              The snow
breathes:
                    mask of sleep, mask of waking.

The gulls are phantoms, drifted into April
from an August field, and in their wake
                    a flash of heat, and dreamy
indolence.
                    The geese on the river island
lie like dark, misshapen loaves.
Catching the blast and bark and laugh
of their tumult,
                         of each tuneless
horn in turn, you can't see which
instrument, all the birds
                              inert. The flaring
alchemical wind is a lung

or a sail.
       And is this, your human shape, more
definite?
       Try for a passable channel
between dogwood and willow,
the trail heavy with grains of what could be
salt or sleep.
       Just about here, just about
yesterday, you saw crocuses, tightly furled
and furred against these predictable
but unforecast
           contingencies.

Remember the other years, other
springs? The diffuse, ashy-blue and always-first
flower, blooming in sleet, in rain, in every
shade of indifferent weather.
           Today's spring
is nominal, a pretence, faint lustering sun
              a smear, grease
on the lens.

Such a short walk, from April to August:
the gulls' cries, a field of wheat,
the wind a mask of sleep.
         The clouds,
ragged now, are slit, and there it is,
a shock of high, vertiginous blue.
           Look now—
              one gust

and it's gone, nothing but static
above the icy water.

White sky, white road. How difficult
to locate the known, the desired
                              entrance,
as the storm inhales through your spine, exhales
through the crown of your skull,
you seem to float, spindrift in a whiteout,
as you turn homeward, as you turn away,
haloed, charged,
                    a breath
between thresholds,
                    unharboured.

River Edge:

now that the snow in the mountains
has ceased melting, the river's drawn in
its skirts, leaving us this gleaming

muck, a shore between sagging banks of ice
and the cold heave of current. April sun
lapping at the phosphorescence

in everything—orange weight on a lost
lure, rusted hook in the river lip, cracked
shells, slick, green-eyed stones—

all skeletal, sleeked and gnarled
by the river mouth. My boots weighted
with clay, I trek downriver, gripping

and skidding along the oozing sand.
With each quarter mile the sun
grows warmer, and fractious, contending

for every branch and bottle cap, every splinter
of day-glow plastic. Nothing is more beautiful
than anything else: this is how April warns us

and breaks us down. Upslope,
the dry-docked hulk of ice sheet, a study
in the structure of the washed-up

and winterkilled. Downslope, the river,
a loosened tongue, icy harangue, coughing
and singing over stones, eddying in the bends

and then surging on. The ice
is riddled, layers of collapsing spindles
clotted with grit, each slab eaten away

from underneath, a cave where the river
wintered. I mind the edge,
balancing between not looking up and not

plunging in. Boot top, surface shimmer, scrolling
wave hem. The floes are dimming shelves,
spent chandelier glass

I kick my way through. Three miles of slog
until the shore is drowned in a spill of roots
and rock, and I'm barred. The wind's

torqued to the north and the sun's downshifted,
blanketing the west in shadow. Turning,
I see the far shore, a mirage,

spotlit, while on this bank, I ride the border
between cold and colder, disorder
and disorder, a painstaking

retraction, stammering toward home and its one
original idea, fire
enchained. All the way back,

the sky lowers, flooding to the horizon
with cloud, darkening the line
between ice and water.

Torch River

The trees are in motion again, swaying,
shaking off dreams.
                            The dream of the lover
lying in state, of the stranger, swift
in pursuit,
                    the dream of height,
of skimming the crowns of trees along the ridge
and looking down as a figure hurries
from nowhere to nowhere,
                                    in snow,
in rain, in a cloak of cold,
wet leaves.

~

Who is she? Impossible to tell
at this distance. Is she lost
or is she at home
walking this tract of mixed forest,
her pockets filled with seeds,
three bright blue feathers
and a bird skull.
                        Or it may be
she carries little but a comb, a ticket
stub, a ring of heavy,
                            polished keys.
Whoever she is,
                    she grows smaller
as the sisterhood of trees, aspen
and birch, sway
                    in the eye

of the nighthawk, unfolding
lengthwise on its branch, taking wing
out of a cloudless sleep.

~

She has stripped off her shirt,
she has tied her hair back—
                              she dares,
in this late, unseasonably tender light
to be flesh.
              She knows
she should be careful, this far down
in the valley, the trail streaked with bear
scat, carved by the slow meander of doe
and fawn.
              She knows she should mind
her directions and have to hand
her compass,
              her knife.
Passing so close to the river, she can hear
its murmurous eddy as she walks, forgetful
of her way in the fragrant noon, her skin
with and of the air, the sun
a light lather, a froth of heat.
She should be wary, prepared,
alert,
        but she isn't, she's kneeling,
her hand spread over the right
foreprint of doe,
                    then fawn.

Her shirt is on the ground and her own
spoor under and around it,
                              one track
overlaying another as she circles,
eyes down, her prints
the mark of an animal without design
                    or destination,
without stealth.

~

The last leaves, thrashing overhead, wild
in the wild upper branches, in a wind
which does not reach her, walking
in twilight,
                at the faltering
hour, her sight fraying
as shadows seep in around her, and nothing
to choose
                between the way ahead,
the same
                narrowing thread,
as the way back.

~

She hesitates, wondering if she should cross
at the old bridge, and weave through
pine,
        or turn inland
with the aspen, to follow their exemplary
flow,
        shoulder to shoulder to shoulder,
the wind tying them together,
                        nothing more
and nothing less,
                each gust
exhaustive,
        and not one
false move.

~

Poised on the river's vanishing
edge, she listens as first snow hisses
through the skeletal roses, the alder,
                        dark ridge
overhead, dark water below.
She balances, arms flung wide, on the lip of white,
on the rough riparian slope and its slip
of new snow, the light
                scant
and shallow, and under it,
the still wakeful
earth,

a layer of sand, a layer of humus,
a layer of clay.

~

Never mind.
        This is not a story.
There is no beginning
and no end.
        The seeds,
forgotten in the inner lining,
will surprise her, years later,
when she shakes them out,
                the dust
they have become.
And the keys were only keys,
scored by daily use,
        they open
but do not release.

~

How long will she stand, swayed by a river
she can't see, in her caul
of snow?
　　　　　Never mind, this is not a dream
but a reckoning. She'll awaken
amidst the trees that hold the night back
in a high arc,
　　　　　　　and she, a ghost
in the grey trough, will want out of that
ravine.
　　　　But first, she'll find
that the river means to stay
as it goes,
　　　　　　that it's deeper
at night, a throat
　　　　　　　　　　sheathed in silt, the current
occult,
　　　　a few faint notes catching
as it sweeps into the next bend.
And she'll hear it,
　　　　　　　　the singing
that walks behind
　　　　　　　　and through her,
as she climbs back out.

Acknowledgements

Some of these poems have appeared previously in *The Malahat Review*, *Grain*, *Prairie Fire*, *The Fiddlehead* and *The River King* in the U.S., and in the anthology *Listening With the Ear of the Heart* (St. Peter's Press, 2003, Margoshes and Sopher, editors). The poem "Fatherhood" was broadcast as "The Mira Poems" on CBC Saskatchewan's program Gallery. Thank you to Kelley Jo Burke, producer, and to actor Kent Allen for his pitch perfect rendering of the poems. The poem "The Waiting Room" was honed in anticipation of a performance as one of a series of "Inhibitions," performances that took place in private spaces in Saskatoon, in March, 2004. With thanks to Dawna Rose for inviting me to participate.

"The Hanging Tree" is for my mother and father, and Jake, the horse.
"Nocturne" is for my mother, with love and thanks for the late night vigils.
"Fatherhood" is for Christopher, Annelise, Mira and Rowan.

Part Three of this collection is in memory of Gail Youngberg.

I am very thankful to the Saskatchewan Arts Board and the Canada Council for the Arts for financial support during the writing of this book. Thanks also to the Saskatchewan Writers Guild's Writers and Artists Colonies for retreat time, and to *Grain* magazine for lessons learned.

Thanks to George and Jean Lidster, Torch Valley Country Retreats, for their consummate hospitality (www.torchvalleycountryretreats.com).

Thank you to Dianne Warren, Connie Gault and Marlis Wesseler for collegial nights of wine and conversation. Thanks in particular to Connie for the title suggestion. Thanks to Lorna Crozier and Patrick Lane for their enduring friendship and faith. Thanks to Don McKay for his incendiary influence. Thanks especially to Tonja Gunvaldsen Klaassen for the "Crocus" correspondence, a vital exchange. To Sylvia Legris for her astute and mischievous mind, and to Jennifer Still for the pleasure of the *Grain* years. Thanks to Patricia Dewar for the gift of "Breath" and her body of wisdom.

Thank you to Jan Zwicky for her insight at a crucial phase in the composition of "Prelude," and thanks again to Jan for her generous and acute editorial comments. Thanks to Kitty and Maureen of Brick Books for shepherding the book through the production process.

Thank you, as always and ever, to Doris Wall Larson, first and last reader, and to Jasmine, master of the art of concentration.

Elizabeth Philips is the author of three collections of poetry, most recently *A Blue with Blood in it* and *Beyond my Keeping*. Both collections received the Saskatchewan Poetry Award for their respective years. She has edited numerous poetry collections and has taught creative writing in the Banff Wired Studio, the Banff Writing Studio, the Banff Writing with Style program, and the Sage Hill Writing Experience. She edited the literary magazine *Grain* from 1998 to 2003. Philips lives in Saskatoon.